Acknowledgements

Editor
Mikka Gilbert
Write Right, LLC

Cover
Thaddeus W. Jones Jr.
Fanatik Productions, LLC

Carrington

To My Readers

First, I would like to thank all of my readers and supporters. I hope that through these words you can enter my bedroom and feel the intenseness of my erotic mind. If after reading each poem you feel warm and wet, ready to jump into bed, and have rough or passionate sex, then that means I have done my job. ENJOY!

www.ingramcontent.com/pod-product-compliance
Lightning Source LLC
Chambersburg PA
CBHW071932020426
42331CB00010B/2835

Now all systems are go, and in motion and running

conductively,

All of this is because I wanted you sexual

and........seductively.

Carrington

Déjà vu

"How bad do you want it?" She asked. I sighed with pleasure
and replied,

'Let's take this conversation outside.'

I tell her I want to fuck her in every open space,

By the pool, the patio, and the outdoor fireplace.

Her eyes began to burn with passion reaching the temps of
hell,

I drop to my knees running my hands up her dress, the heat
between them and her skin left a scorching trail.

I use my middle finger to move her pink thongs out of my way;

her pussy's dripping with approval and desperation,

The rhythmic sound of my fingers inside of her claims her
sight, her pupils dilated with delectation.

For a moment she forgot who she was, her moans become
incoherent,

I'm putting her pussy through pleasurable torture in ways undoubtedly indifferent.

She cries out, "I need you to fuck me; I'm ready to cum, fuck me hard with your extended dick!"

I oblige, putting my back into it, to the likes of the both of us I am apolaustic.

I'm pumping her, pounding her with my steel giving her sexual absolution,

Her pussy is feeling pleasurable pain while, I keep hitting her G-spot with a force of intrusion.

She sits up and digs her chocolate painted nails in my back,

Her toes are curled because she is ready to climax.

She screams, "I love the way you fuck me, no one can keep taking me to this place of grace as you do!"

Even though I never fuck her the same way, I still give her that sense of sexual deja vu.

Carrington

Miracle

Allow me a moment to be provocative,

With just my voice if you will, to be evocative.

Allow me a moment with your eyes closed,

Read verb to your body as it is written prose.

Allow me a moment to make you make a sound so tumultuous that it will confuse the neighbors,

Because the sexual chemistry between two women has many flavors and need no favors.

Allow me to submerse myself in you and then walk across your waters,

Allow me to be the doctor that heals you and fill all of your orders.

Allow me to be the one dominating and physical,

Allow me to be the knight, the lord in your bed to perform a sexual miracle.

Sexual Domination

You think I am a goody-good, but I have not let you know more than you should. I wanted to leave things to your imagination, so that all else I reveal would come as a surprise in a later presentation. First, I want to fuck you between your breasts until your chest starts to sweat and your pussy gets wet. Then, I will use my mouth to eat you out to end your sex-craving drought with the flow of your natural juices. You will need each and every one of them for their natural uses. Why? I keep your legs spread across the bed because to the domain of multiple orgasms and body spasms are where we're headed. And when this comes into play, you'll already be a million worlds away sucking and salivating on my dildo. As the intensity level of our fuck sessions begins to grow, the aggression begins to flow. Our bodies begin to make preparations for my dildo's penetration as we cross the line of kinky sex into sexual domination.

Carrington

Come

Come be with me so I can set you free and put you in a daze,

Come be with me to make every part of you burn fiercely,

burn, burning, ablaze.

Come be with me and let me take your body in my bosom to

be awakened,

Come be with me so that I settle down the parts of you that

have been shaken.

Come be with me so that I can arouse all of your senses,

Come be with me so that I can break down your barriers and

defenses.

Come be with me so that I can take you out of the shadows

and make you my silhouette,

Come be with me so that I can intoxicate you with the natural

use of sex.

Popsicle

I see her; the beauty of her body captures me and turns on my inner beast,

Locked in ready to pounce, primitive, like a lion, I am ready to feast.

She catches eye contact with me like she's ready to feed my appetite so immense,

I'm ready to ravish every part of her that's lavish, in a manner so intense.

I've got to show her that I have ways are animalistic, yet artistic and intrusive,

That will leave her expressing feelings that are uncontrollably effusive.

I want to make her cum so much until it begins to trickle,

Then lick up all juices that has melted from her pussy's popsicle.

Carrington

Sexual Science

Like the moon, I have a direct effect on your waves,

When I'm inside of your sexual tides, I am often in a daze.

I am like the earth's plates, when I shift, your body quakes,

Like a Tsunami, I create abrupt movements in your ocean's floor,

Like a wild fire, I make you burn with passion from my strokes of lightning that puts your body in a heated uproar.

Like an eclipse when I kiss your lips, I turn your day into night,

As the winds of a tornado, I can make your world spin on a different axis,

When I love you just right.

Crown Me

I try to sleep but I can't because her body is unveiled and with it,

I want to be sexually and explosively explicit.

I kissed her from the nape of her neck down to the small of her back trying not to wake her, but she smells so aromatically fragrant,

Even in her sleep I force words out of her that are so flagrant.

She feels the touch of my fingers linger on her skin sending a course desire down her body and around her erected clit,

Trying to control the flow of her juices, I can't let her do this so I begin to effectively lick.

She grabs at my locks and says, "Please don't stop!" I feel her beginning to heave,

The more I lick her, her pussy and body are both dancing and vying with my tongue, the heavier she pants, the faster she breathes.

I'm fucking her so good she begins to turn and twist,

Like in her former life she was a tensile contortionist.

I could feel the expanding and contracting of her cervix,

Ready for me to fuck it every way I know how to reach its vertex.

The way she lets me fuck her sends ripples through my body like a chain reaction,

Carrington

After all, I am known to be the king of sexual abstraction and she the queen of action and distraction.

The next thing I heard her say was, "I don't want to cum while you're going down on me,"

Aggressively she flips over on top of me and with her pussy she enveloped and crowned me.

Fifty Shades of Gay

Some women are raving about, "Fifty Shades of Grey,"

Others are craving me and the way I play.

With their Body,

While like Shirley Murdock's, "As We Lay."

I don't need whips and chains to sustain, or ascertain,

The sensual spots of your body that are in my sight so plain.

All I need is my tongue, prismatic,

Moving in all Directions so systematic to make your screams dramatic,

While you're awake, your body dreams of me as I Attack it with my sexual tactics.

Does your body want more? I don't have to ask it,

Even with clothes on it can't mask it.

It needs my touch so fantastic,

That it stretches every Part of you like its elastic.

Carrington

As I give you my rubber and plastic, leaving your body so ecstatic,

When I'm gone, for you this is problematic.

Sexual Prophet

I want to be so deep in you that you will confess it, that you'll want me to change every part of you, down to your genetics. Your body, I will bless it, I want to be the D.N.A. that runs through you, not just your genetics, but your metrics that means "Damn Near All" of you every time I call to you. I want to be so far in you that I am playing with your body behind the scenes if you know what I mean. Nothing about the words I seek to speak is clean, and nothing about the way I sneak a peek into your jeans is discreet. Now we both are in a place unseen, hidden in a love making scheme, even in your dreams. I will leave you numb like I'm your personal anesthetic; my energy will run through you like it is kinetic as I whisper sweet nothings, oh so poetic. I speak these things to come as if they are already done. I make us become as one because I am sexually prophetic.

Carrington

Your Candy Factory

Let me Hershey Kiss your lips and taste all the pieces of

your Reese's. Let me be the one who Charms you until I set

the alarms off in you like an Atomic Fireball. Let me feel the

sweet softness of your Werther's Original. I want to taste the

riddles of your Skittles and take a ride on your twists of Twix.

Let me lick up the sugary cum of your Pixie Sticks. I eat up

the M&Ms you left on the trail to your mix, but never using

my Chick-O-Stick. Let me lay between your legs so I can

connect your Dots. Let me suck on your clitoris in your Kit

Kat like a cherry Blow Pop, to send you into another day in

the Milky Way. Let me continue to fuck you until you curse

because I made your Starburst. Now call me your Sugar

Daddy since I've brought you Almond Joy, by playing in your

Fun Dip and sucking on your Nik-L Nips. As a result, we can

make a new candy……Oh-Boy.

Aries

I am the Aries that comes in a form so rare,

That in the midst of my presence leaves you gasping for air.

I am easily turned on by stimulating conversation,

And long talks of sexual simulation.

I am one to set the ambiance,

With incense and scented candles in a beautiful sconce.

I am one who will engage in a sensual love making epic,

that's my preference,

I am one that with me you can experience several passionate

quickies that need no reference.

I am audacious, like a dragon, I am an impetuous fire filled

creature,

Carrington

I am one who often initiates sex, ready to reveal all of its

features.

I am in myself, along with my words that serve as a natural

aphrodisiac,

When your body aligns with my sign, we change the name of

the zodiac.

Daydream

Somewhere in the day I get lost in the clouds, thinking of you half naked and unbloused,

I get aroused.

It's like my mind is in a spellbinding attraction of you,

On its own rendezvous.

It feels so real that my fingertips sweat like they're feeling the creamy moistness of your milk,

Caught in the lust of your opalescent web, your pussy begins to feel like silk.

I got so tangled in you that I started giving you the best of me, fucking you recklessly,

Fucking you in the sill of the window for the neighbors to see.

I watch them watch us and wink. They stare in awe, the husband's jacking off; the wife drops her jaw fingering herself and mouthing, "Fuck me."

I'm fucking you with such finesse, touching all of your body's fragments,

You surrender, your body weakening with such acquiescence.

I try to move you away from the window; you grab the sill and say, "Let them see, I don't want to be obscure,"

Carrington

I asked if you're sure, you said, "Yes," in a way that was so demure.

You kept saying, "Taste me; drink from the stream of my cream!"

But before my lips could touch yours, I awakened from the daydream.

Tunnel Vision

Your beauty within itself has a way of setting my soul on fire,

Your body fills my thirst and all that it requires.

The smoothness of your skin quenches my desires,

That keeps me coming back for more, as I am your only frequent flyer.

Your eyes captivate me, fascinates me, in ways I cannot mention,

Your spirit puts my spirit in a sacred place, like the stars in their ascension.

Your hand in mine, every time, takes me to another dimension,

Your light in my light will always have my attention.

Carrington

Musical Instrument

I kissed her lips, her neck, and licked the sweat beads from her chest. Her breasts, she arched them towards my mouth. I invite them, entice them, and pushed three fingers inside of her, with pleasure. She is dissolved; with each finger stroke she becomes more involved. I drive my tongue inside her of setting off a shattering chord of music. I play her body like every stringed instrument, finely tuned, so acoustic. The strings of her screams make the most glorious sounds. She repositions herself to sit on my fingers, fucking herself in a counter clockwise motion, up and down, up and down. She whispers, "I want you to move closer to my lower." I do so to taste her absolute deliciousness, plundering her with my tongue; I crooked it to hit her spot turning her high pitched moans into an orgasm as she cums. Now I have in that instance broken down the sexual resistance she had been showing. I look up to see her satisfied and her face glowing.

Sequence of My Tongue

I have a tongue that can get and keep you sprung; that can

bring both pleasure and wreak havoc,

I have a tongue that even when you don't want it, parts of you

have to have it.

I have a tongue that can bind you and everything around you,

better than whips and chains,

A tongue that will surround you and you're happy I found you

because it keeps you tamed.

I have a tongue of steel that is sexually lethal, so

exceptionally complex; it will leave you wanting the sequel,

Because each time will never be the same and neither time

will be equal.

Carrington

Kiss of Illusion

The taste of her is as tender as her touch, so succulent and divine.

The kiss of her lips is delicate and sweet, her beauty aged, fine as wine.

Every part of her I own, as if I created her to only be mine. I want to taste the rum of her plums with the finesse of my tongue that leaves me drunken with bliss,

Her absence leaves me in a state of confusion, as she leaves behind the illusion of her kiss.

Unspoken Words

I put my finger over her lips and tell her not to speak a word,

She looks at me in disbelief like she couldn't believe what

she'd just heard.

I motion her to come over; she moves closer, her head, she

rests upon my chest,

Gently I move her, to fit the groove of her. She moans quietly,

I then decidedly begin to caress her breasts.

She says, "Talk to me sexually."

Again, I tell her, don't say a word.

So that my hands can get lost in deep conversation,

With her body's translation.

The reason I tell her not to speak is so I can keep my

concentration,

To focus on curing her of her sexual and sleep deprivation.

Tonight all she'll need is me and poetry to make the mood

lighter.

Her body will be my paper, and my tongue her best writer.

Carrington

After Her Hours

A long day of work her face reads of nothing but frustration, until she comes home to me to place her body in deep meditation and relaxation. I lead her to the bathroom, undress her, mirrors fogged from the heat of the bubble bath, filling the air with the smell of strawberries and champagne, Candles surround the tub, dimly lit while I give her a shoulder rub. She closes her eyes and sips on the sparkling wine that I left chilling, to help take the stress away she had been feeling. After I bathe her in my love, she lays down on our plush white comforter, then I begin to rub soothing lotions on her. She lays on the rose petals I designed in the shape of a heart. She eats the chocolate covered infused strawberries, and cherries. She smiles and says, "You're smart." After her hours I treat her like royalty. After her hours, I make love to her, treating her like the angel she is to me.

Hidden Pleasure

I come with a secret, and if you can keep it, you would have

found the golden treasure,

Like how I will go to any measure to bring my woman every

pleasure.

The way I study her body language,

Revealing the frustration she's concealing from her sexual

anguish.

I brush my hand across her face and place the other at the

small of her back,

To pull her close to me like we're in a motion picture ready to

act.

In Act 1, I show her that to no other I cannot be

characterized,

In Act 2 with the touch of my hands, I get her aroused and

energized.

Carrington

In Act 3, she will see how I can leave a woman in wonder,

In Act 4, she asks for more, now I have permission to explore her while I pin her hands down acting on my intensions to go under.

In Act 5, she realizes that the way I handle a woman cannot be plagiarized,

It's not written in the words of a book only imprinted on her leaving her mesmerized,

By Act 6, well, I will leave it like this....because I've never been one to ruin a surprise.

Her Life: The Series

Inspired by: Phoenix Griffin

Carrington

The Initiation

She gets out of the shower and I stare at her nakedness in its

full length. I grab her and lift her against the wall for her to

feel my strength. The imprint of my physique pressed against

hers in ways that are unique. My body surged into hers until I

was deep in her sweet heat, submerged! I could feel her

hormones percolate; her heart racing like it's insane. I could

hear her blood humming with pleasure through her veins. I

lift her legs around my hips and insert myself into her life.

She feels so good that I think I want to make her my wife. My

strokes get harder and smoother as she gets wetter and

wetter; she arches her back away from the wall to receive me

better. While I'm banging and beguiling her, licking her neck

with my tongue, her body beckoned me like a sirens song...

The Release

Over my shoulders, she draped her arm, holding me, squeezing me tighter and tighter. The pace of her breathing becomes lighter and lighter. Her body I placed in my sexual restraints, she bites her bottom lip like she's trying to hold her own constraints. She doesn't want me to know that the rough way I am exploring her life is just what she wants, with her not imploring me to feed and exceed her needs. So engulfed in her tides, I didn't realize that the walls of her life clinched tightly to me while I was inside trying to hold me captive in its unadulterated prison. Her climax is steadily rising, rising...risen. Her life is trembling filled with lust, adrenaline, endorphins, and me. I'm slaying her and swaying her. I know because her life is leaking steadily. Her climax came in drugging waves, she lets out a cry of release, and her life is left in chaos with no peace.

Carrington

The Aftermath

Now I hold her as she uncontrollably slides down the wall. Her legs, tightly clenched, her life drenched. It was like her life tried to control itself, trying to retrench. She moved her right hand to touch her life because I know I have erupted its uterine lining. She begins passionately pining with anticipation of our lives again intertwining. I watch as her life and her body both still shaking, still writhing. Her life like the muscles of her body was frozen then exploded. As a result, her body was being rocked. Her trembles become waves of mini aftershocks. Her life is still having orgasms and spasms in the order of twos and threes. Her life is still in shock that it was just pleased by a human trapeze.

The Intermission

After her life has received its fix from my dick, I help her on to her feet. She looks into my eyes still drunken, and said, "We may need to get some sleep." She doesn't know that I want more of her life, driving into it deep. The things that I did to her life could get me life because I followed no letter of legalism. I did it all in the name of her life's hedonism. She managed to slur and say, "I almost feel as if you drugged me." I said, "No, I left your eyes dilated and merely intoxicated as we crossed the line of decency." I tucked her in, gently kissing her cheek then turned off the light. The last thing she said before she drifted to sleep was, "How did we get this all in on one night...?"

Carrington

The Invitation

The next morning I awakened to her staring at me, like I'm her heroic Adonis and she a cougar, but yet a Vixen. Her eyes glistening like she's ready to strike, knowing that if she does, it will be her life that gets stricken. As I lie on my back she sits on top of me. Her life is on mine at the same time. She's rubbing and squeezing her breasts, pleasuring herself as if it is me she is taunting. It seems that the ghost of last night's past is still in her life and still haunting. She lifts just a little and begins to play with her life, grinding and gyrating on top of me. Her life is still vulnerable to my touch, so palpably. I can feel from the vibrations and pulsations of her life that it wanted me in a way so different that I followed its persuasions of fulfillment. ...so I accept its invitation. Her life began speaking though her telling me it wants all I have, all the lust and love of me. She translated that her life felt it had not had all there was of me. She leans forward for her face to meet mine and she turns her head slightly to the right. She pulls my mouth to her neck and whispers one word, "Bite!" I do so leaving my teeth marks like love notes written on her flesh. She takes in a deep breath; this seems to give her life back its life, replenished and refreshed. Her life now in control, overtaking her body, she pushes my head down and to my face she begins to crawl. Her life is leaving a trail of its wetness; I brace myself to answer its call. The next thing I know her life is even to my face, I bring my mouth up to meet it. I can hear her frantically grasping and clasping the headboard of the bed, she yells out, "Oh my God fuck my life! Eat it! Eat it!" In an instant, her life is in control fucking itself with my mouth piece. It goes in directions not known to a man, for my tongue to feel it's every crease. I open my mouth wider and wider to get more of my tongue inside her so that in her life's climax I can make an impact. That was the day I made her life peak twice, leak twice, and drank of its erotic extract.

Carrington

Phone Play

Since our sexual encounter, a few days have passed. She hadn't heard from me. I received a text that read, "Why haven't you called?" followed by, "Not speaking to me is absurd of you to me." I smile and chuckle to myself. She says she's counting down my hours to leave work. She sends me a text and a picture of her life as an added perk. The caption on this picture was, "Baby, hurry up!" I thought, hmm, should I be nice to her and leave? Nah, I'd rather entice her, leaving her life to believe that it won't be pleased. I opened my desk drawer and sent a picture of my plastic stem, only sending a caption of two words… "Imagine them." Though she knows I am at work she calls, I answer, she says, "Just listen." She places the phone close to her life, playing with it, making sounds, swishing and squishing. I can feel her life climax peaking, her pheromones seeping and speaking through the phone. Her breathing gets quiet; I say, "Hello?" and she lets

out a moan. She's chanting and panting, "Please come to me,

my life is panicking!" I grab my keys and run out the door,

knowing her life needs a masculine handling. I cranked my

car, the phone still to my ear. Her words are slurred and

rambling. I throw my phone in the passenger seat on speaker.

I floor my car as she's calling out for me. Fixed on trying to

get to her, I'm not answering...

Carrington

The Seductress

Ten minutes, I am at her door banging on it like I'm about to bang her. She opens the door in a sexual rage that is no longer strange to her. She stands there like she's ready to seduce in a silk robe embroidered with the name Seductress, she left it un-sashed. I draw her close to me eagerly, grasping her round, brown ass. I'm kissing her, backing her into the room. I lift her on top of the dresser. Her life begins to sing my praises because it knows I am about to bless her. I lean her back and push myself inside of her life, playing with the heart of it with my thumb. My other hand, I use to hold her in place to ensure she doesn't run. Her life makes it difficult for me to make love to her, so I aggressively fuck it. With one of her hands she's playing with one of her breasts. I move it out of the way so I can suck it! Pounding the on the flesh of her life she goes into a state of nirvana. Heavily we breathe, profusely sweating; her life was hot like a sauna. I whisper in

her ear that we're about to have a different scene of sex. She

says, "Bring it baby, I wanna!" Speaking through the gritting

of her teeth, thrusting her life against mine she asks, "What's

next?" Never pulling out of her, I lift her and carry her to the

balcony; she puts her leg up on the rail. I've never seen her

so pale, her actions so conducive. In this position, her life

seems to go in another direction like it's trying to be elusive.

She didn't know I'm exclusively adept, and her life cannot

escape. I was fucking her long, deep, and strong that her life

felt inept and called it consensual rape. I take her from the

balcony's rail and bend her over the patio table putting her in

a disadvantaged position. Pushing up the cushion of her ass

cheeks, I spread them. With no hands, I put in my stem,

embedding them like I'm wedding them. Her life is so wet that

I am sliding out, so I slow down and stoke deeply just enough

Carrington

for her life to ride it out. I had to prove to her life that I wasn't done and that I had one more trick up my sleeve. I turn her over on the table flat on her back, putting her legs on my shoulders up to her knees. I put my hands behind her back and under her shoulders to keep her steady, to hold her, and to keep my leverage. I fucked her life and fucked her life. She came and let a seductress scream out; I pulled out in enough time to drink of her life's beverage.

www.ingramcontent.com/pod-product-compliance
Lightning Source LLC
Chambersburg PA
CBHW071743020426
42331CB00008B/2156